IT'S TIME TO EAT SUBMARINE SANDWICH

It's Time to Eat SUBMARINE SANDWICH

Walter the Educator

Silent King Books
A WhichHead Entertainment Imprint

Copyright © 2024 by Walter the Educator

All rights reserved. No part of this book may be reproduced in any manner whatsoever without written per- mission except in the case of brief quotations embodied in critical articles and reviews.

First Printing, 2024

Disclaimer

This book is a literary work; the story is not about specific persons, locations, situations, and/or circumstances unless mentioned in a historical context. Any resemblance to real persons, locations, situations, and/or circumstances is coincidental. This book is for entertainment and informational purposes only. The author and publisher offer this information without warranties expressed or implied. No matter the grounds, neither the author nor the publisher will be accountable for any losses, injuries, or other damages caused by the reader's use of this book. The use of this book acknowledges an understanding and acceptance of this disclaimer.

It's Time to Eat SUBMARINE SANDWICH is a collectible early learning book by Walter the Educator suitable for all ages belonging to Walter the Educator's Time to Eat Book Series. Collect more books at WaltertheEducator.com

USE THE EXTRA SPACE TO TAKE NOTES AND DOCUMENT YOUR MEMORIES

SUBMARINE SANDWICH

It's lunchtime now, oh, what a wish!

It's Time to Eat
Submarine Sandwich

A submarine sandwich, so big and delish.

Layered with goodies, so long and wide,

A yummy adventure waiting inside!

First comes the bread, soft or so crisp,

Baked to perfection, oh, what a twist!

It's shaped like a boat, a floating dream,

To hold all the flavors, the sandwich supreme.

Lettuce so crunchy, green and fresh,

Tomatoes so juicy, the very best.

Cheese in slices, melty and neat,

Stacked with care, it's ready to eat!

Add some meat, like turkey or ham,

Or maybe roast beef, oh yes, you can!

Some love chicken or tuna fish,

So many choices, it's your dish!

It's Time to Eat
Submarine Sandwich

Cucumbers, pickles, peppers, too,

Pile them high, it's all up to you.

A drizzle of mustard, or mayo to spread,

A burst of flavor with each bite ahead!

"What's in yours?" asks little Lee,

"Mine has some avocado, come and see!"

"No onions for me," says sister Sue,

"Just extra cheese and a pickle or two!"

Bite after bite, the fun begins,

The submarine sandwich always wins.

It's long and tasty, a meal so grand,

Every bite made with loving hands.

It's perfect for picnics or lunch at school,

A submarine sandwich is always cool.

Fold up the paper, take it to go,

It's Time to Eat

Submarine Sandwich

It's the best companion, rain or snow!

Sharing's the fun when the sandwich is big,

Split it in half, it's a tasty gig.

"Here, take a piece," we laugh and play,

The joy of a sub brightens the day.

So when it's time for a lunch that's great,

A submarine sandwich is worth the wait.

With layers of love, it's quite a feat,

It's Time to Eat
Submarine Sandwich

A delicious delight we're ready to eat!

ABOUT THE CREATOR

Walter the Educator is one of the pseudonyms for Walter Anderson. Formally educated in Chemistry, Business, and Education, he is an educator, an author, a diverse entrepreneur, and he is the son of a disabled war veteran. "Walter the Educator" shares his time between educating and creating. He holds interests and owns several creative projects that entertain, enlighten, enhance, and educate, hoping to inspire and motivate you. Follow, find new works, and stay up to date with Walter the Educator™

at WaltertheEducator.com

www.ingramcontent.com/pod-product-compliance
Lightning Source LLC
LaVergne TN
LVHW010411070526
838199LV00064B/5263